MAKE
PAPER LANTERN
ANIMALS

by the editors of Klutz

KLUTZ®

CONTENTS

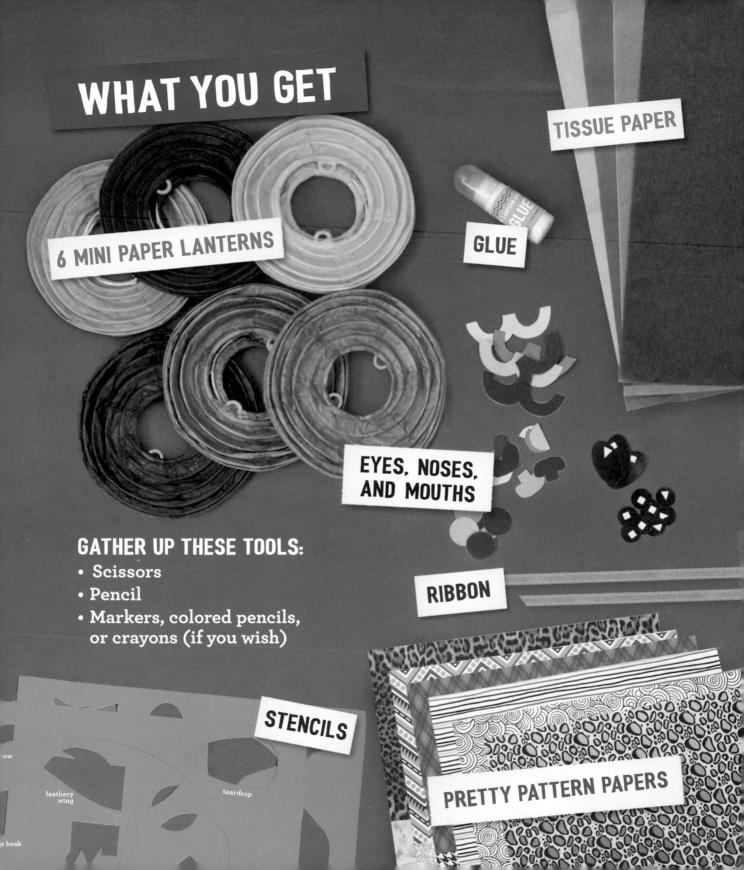

WHAT YOU GET

TISSUE PAPER

6 MINI PAPER LANTERNS

GLUE

EYES, NOSES, AND MOUTHS

GATHER UP THESE TOOLS:
- Scissors
- Pencil
- Markers, colored pencils, or crayons (if you wish)

RIBBON

STENCILS

feathery wing

teardrop

beak

ow

PRETTY PATTERN PAPERS

BUILDING YOUR LANTERN

Whether you're making a sweet kitten or a majestic lion, every project starts by building a lantern.

1 Pick the color for the base of your animal. Look at the pictures for ideas or invent a totally new design.

2 Place the lantern on a flat surface, with the two little rings facing up.

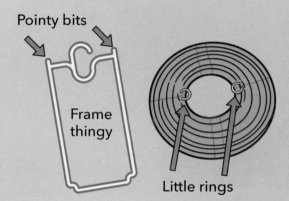

Pointy bits

Frame thingy

Little rings

3 Hold the frame thingy so that the top (the hanging end) is upright and the bottom bar fits inside the lantern's bottom hole. Make sure the bar is centered in the hole.

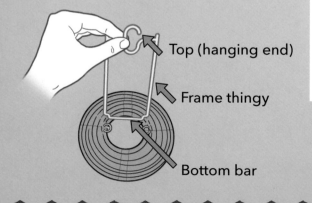

Top (hanging end)

Frame thingy

Bottom bar

■ Make sure you have the wire centered across the bottom of the lantern.

■ Pull the lantern up slowly and carefully.

■ If you're having trouble, find an adult assistant to help you.

Lanterns are delicate and can rip easily. Always handle with care.

4 Slowly and carefully, pull the papery part of the lantern up and around the frame thingy.

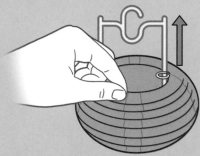

5 Stretch the lantern and slide the rings over the pointy bits on the frame thingy, one at a time.

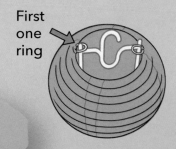

First one ring

Then the other ring

OH NO, MY LANTERN RIPPED!

Maybe you were just excited about starting the craft, or you've been working out too hard in gym class. If you accidentally make a tear in your paper lantern, there are a few ways to fix it:

◾ Cover it up with a strategically placed decoration.

◾ Glue a little patch of tissue paper in a matching color.

◾ Tell everyone it's a design choice. You meant to do it!

DECORATING

Got your paper lantern assembled? Great! It's ready for your creative touch. Each animal has its own instructions, but here are the basics.

1 At the beginning of each project is a "You Will Need" box. Start by gathering up the stencils listed here.

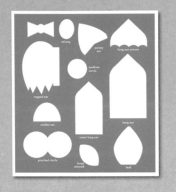

2 Pick out the pretty pattern papers you like from inside the box.

3 Trace the stencils onto the pretty papers lightly with a pencil, and cut out the shape. Try a colored pencil or a marker if your pencil lines don't show.

4 Dot glue on the back of the pretty paper piece and hold it on the lantern until it dries.

Trace patterns near the edge to leave you more paper for other shapes.

Follow the instructions for each animal. You may need to glue a few layers of pretty papers together first, before you add the piece to your lantern.

DISPLAYING

Show off your animal lanterns however you choose.

* **String your lanterns** along the ribbon to make a garland.

* **Tie the ribbon** through the top of a lantern, and hang it from the ceiling or inside a locker.

* **Nestle a lantern** on your desk or nightstand.

* **If you'd like,** place a small battery-operated LED light inside the paper lantern before you hang it up. (Secure it to the bottom bar of the frame thingy with masking tape.) You can find LED lights for lighting up Halloween jack-o'-lanterns. Turn off the lights when you're not using them.

• Always ask an adult if you want to stick something to the wall or hang it from the ceiling. Have a tall adult hang it high enough so you won't bonk your head.

• Animals don't like fire! Never, ever use a candle inside or around your lantern. Make sure to keep the paper away from flames or hot lightbulbs.

• If you have more elaborate schemes in mind for your paper lanterns, ask an adult assistant to help you out.

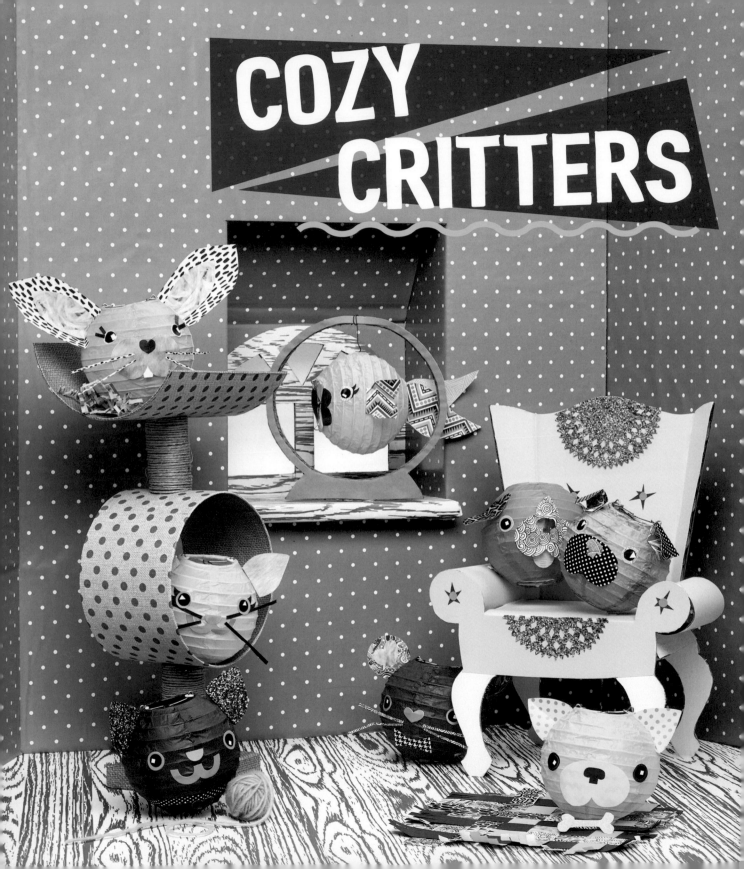

COZY CRITTERS

Puppy

YOU WILL NEED

2 irises

x2

2 pupils

2 leaves

1 mushroom nose

1 muzzle

Do you like dogs with long, droopy ears or short, pointy ears? Mix & match different shapes to create your own custom pup!

1 EARS

Fold each leaf twice, as shown.

2 EYES

Layer one pupil on top of each iris. No one will be able to resist those sweet puppy dog eyes!

3 NOSE

Glue the mushroom nose on top of the muzzle.

4 ALL TOGETHER

Glue all the pieces to your lantern.

Kitten

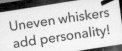

Uneven whiskers add personality!

YOU WILL NEED

- 2 pupils
- 2 irises
- 1 smile
- 2 leaves **x2**
- 1 half circle
- 4 whiskers **x4**
- 2 glam eyes (optional)

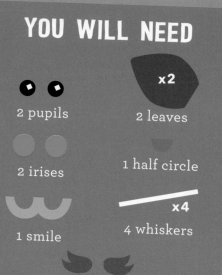

1 EARS
Fold each leaf along the dotted line as shown.

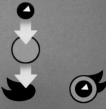

2 EYES
Stack the eye pieces and glue them together in this order, from bottom to top: glam eye, iris, and pupil.

3 NOSE
Place the half circle above the smile and cut out whiskers to go on either side.

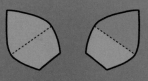

4 ALL TOGETHER
Glue the face to the front of the lantern, and the ears on each side. Meow-velous!

Mouse

This tiny mouse looks dapper with a bow tie or sweet with a hair bow.

1 EARS

Glue a heart to each round ear. Fold along the dotted line as shown to make each ear stand up.

2 FACE

Add a pupil to each iris. Cut long pieces for whiskers.

3 ALL TOGETHER

Stick the heart nose to the center of the lantern, and arrange the eyes, whiskers, and ears as shown.

11

Bunny

1 EARS

First, glue one inner ear to each of the long ears. Fold each ear along the lines as shown. Cut a little line into the bottom fold to make tabs. Then, bring the tabs closer together and add a dab of glue at the inside corner where they meet.

2 EYES

Glue one pupil to each iris.

3 NOSE

Pop the heart nose on top of the dip in the pinched circle and glue the rabbity tooth below. Add long pieces to make whiskers.

YOU WILL NEED

2 pupils	x4 4 whiskers
2 irises	1 pinched circle
x2 2 long ears	1 heart nose
x2 2 inner long ears	1 tooth

4 ALL TOGETHER

Center the nose and cheeks on the lantern. Then add the eyes and ears.

You may need to hold the ears in place as they dry. Make sure the ears are good and dry before hanging your little bunny.

Fish

YOU WILL NEED

2 pupils

1 fish tail

2 glam eyes

2 irises

x2
2 fins

x2
2 hearts

1 TAIL

Fold the fish tail along the dotted line as shown. Thread the tail over the bottom of the frame thingy and add a dot of glue to hold it in place.

2 EYES

Glue the pupil to the iris to the glam eyes, then glue them to the lantern.

3 LIPS

Fold each heart in half. Glue one to each side of the lantern top, to make a pair of fishy lips.

4 FINS

Fold the fins along the lines as shown. Glue one fin to each side of the lantern.

HAPPY CAMPERS

Raccoon

YOU WILL NEED

x2

2 pointy ears

2 almonds

1 mask

1 smile

2 irises

2 pupils

1 oval

1 EARS

Fold each ear along the lines, and snip a short line in the middle as shown. Bring the two bottom edges together, and glue the inner corners where they meet.

2 EYES

Glue the irises to the mask, then glue the pupils on top.

3 ALL TOGETHER

After you add the whole mask with eyes to the lantern, glue two almonds on the forehead, and add the oval nose and a sneaky smile. Don't forget to attach the ears!

Bat

1 EARS

Fold each oval in half and glue a half-circle onto the upper part. They will be the bat's ears.

2 WINGS

Fold each raggedy ear as shown to make the wings.

3 EYES

Create eyes by gluing the pupils to the irises.

4 MOUTH

Glue the tiny triangles behind the smile before you glue the smile to the lantern.

5 ALL TOGETHER

You know what to do! Glue the ears, eyes, nose, mouth, and wings in place.

YOU WILL NEED

2 ovals

2 irises

2 pupils

3 half-circles x3

1 smile

2 triangles

2 raggedy ears x2

Owl

1 BELLY

Start with the shortest scallop, then glue the longer pieces on top, staggering them.

2 EYES

Assemble the eyes in this order from bottom to top: large circle, medium circle, iris, and pupil.

3 FRONT

Glue the belly to the front of the lantern and add the wings so it can fly! *Note: Your lantern can't really fly.*

4 ALL TOGETHER

Glue the two eyes directly onto the lantern above the scallops. Add a beak.

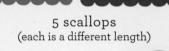

YOU WILL NEED

5 scallops
(each is a different length)

2 medium circles

2 curvy wings
x2

2 irises

1 beak

2 pupils

2 large circles

Deer

YOU WILL NEED

- 2 antlers **x2**
- 2 pupils
- 2 curvy leaves **x2**
- 2 almonds
- 2 small irises
- 2 ovals
- 2 large almonds
- 1 snout
- 1 large pupil

You might want to practice with an easier lantern first. Deer can be a bit fiddly.

1 EARS

Fold the antlers and ears as shown. Glue an almond to the middle of each curvy leaf and fold along the dotted lines.

2 EYES

Layer the eyes from bottom to top: large almond, oval, iris, and pupil.

3 SNOUT

Glue the large pupil to the snout as shown. Bring the two sides of the snout together under the middle flap and glue them together. Pull the middle section down and glue it in place.

4 ALL TOGETHER

Run a line of glue all the way around the inside of the snout, then stick it in place on the lantern. Once the snout is in place, add the eyes, ears, and antlers around it.

1 EARS

Fold, cut, and glue the ears just like the raccoon's on page 15.

2 CHEEKS

Glue the two teardrops together to make a foxy face shape.

3 FACE

Add the half-circle in the center, and the eyes on each side (glue the iris first, then the pupil on top).

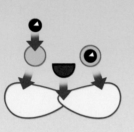

4 TAIL

Glue the fox accent onto the long ear to make a tail.

5 ALL TOGETHER

Place the ears, the face, and the tail on the lantern.

YOU WILL NEED

2 pupils

1 half-circle

2 irises

x2
2 pointy ears

1 long ear

x2
2 tear drops

1 fox accent

PARTY ANIMALS

Flamingo

1 HEAD

Fold tabs on the flamingo heads as shown. Glue the flamingo heads back-to-back so that the tabs stick out.

2 FACE

Glue one flamingo beak to each side of the head, plus eyes (stack the irises on top of the pupils).

3 LEGS

Fold the tab on the legs as shown and wrap the folded tab around the bottom bar of the lantern. Glue it in place.

4 ALL TOGETHER

Position the head on the lantern. Then glue a wing on both sides!

YOU WILL NEED

2 flamingo heads

2 feathery wings

2 flamingo beaks

2 irises

2 pupils

1 flamingo legs

Panda

YOU WILL NEED

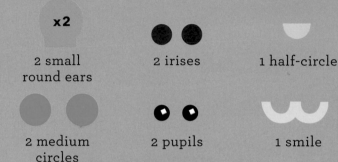

x2

2 small
round ears

2 irises

1 half-circle

2 medium
circles

2 pupils

1 smile

1 EARS

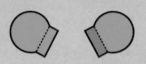

Fold each ear along
the lines as shown.

2 EYES

Create two eyes by
layering these pieces,
from bottom to top:
medium circle, iris,
and pupil.

3 ALL TOGETHER

Assemble the ears
and eyes onto your
lantern. Glue the
smile underneath
the half-circle.

Sea Turtle

1 HEAD

Glue two round ears back-to-back to create the head, and fold the bottom tabs so they stick out. Glue the eyes to each side of the head.

2 FLIPPERS

Fold two of the curvy leaves and glue them as shown to make back flippers. Simply glue the other two flippers to the sides of the lantern.

3 SHELL

Decorate the shell by gluing ovals or circles all around the top of the lantern.

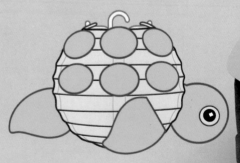

YOU WILL NEED

x14
14 ovals
(more if you'd like)

2 irises

2 pupils

x2
2 large round ears

x4
4 curvy leaves

Tree Frog

YOU WILL NEED

2 medium circles

2 tree frog feet x2

2 large pupils

1 wave

Decorate your frog with little spots for freckles.

1 EYES

Create eyes by gluing a large pupil to the center of each circle.

2 MOUTH

Add the wave to the center of the lantern to make a smile.

3 FEET

Glue the tree frog feet to the bottom of the lantern.

4 ALL TOGETHER

You know what to do next—add those peepers!

Koala

To make a sleepy koala, glue one half-circle on top of each eye so that half the pupil and iris are covered up.

YOU WILL NEED

2 large almonds

2 irises

2 pupils

x2

2 raggedy ears

1 oblong

2 half circles (optional)

1 EARS

Attach one large almond to the center of each raggedy ear. Fold along the lines as shown.

2 EYES

Create eyes by gluing a pupil onto each iris. *(See the tip in the box to make sleepy eyes.)*

3 ALL TOGETHER

Place the oblong in the center to make a nose, and then add the eyes on each side.

Lion

1 EARS

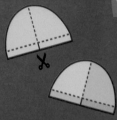

Fold each ear along the dotted lines as shown. Bring the inner corners together and glue them in place.

2 EYES

Create an eye by gluing these shapes in this order, from bottom to top: oval, iris, and pupil.

3 NOSE

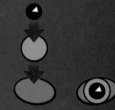

Glue the beak shape to the dip in the pinched circle to create a muzzle.

4 ALL TOGETHER

After you glue the face and ears in place, cut lots of leaves out of tissue paper. You need about 26 to make a full lion's mane. Glue them in place in a ring around the lantern, making sure to glue some behind the ears.

YOU WILL NEED

2 stubby ears **x2**

2 pupils

2 ovals

1 beak

2 irises

26 curvy leaves **x26**
(use tissue paper)

1 pinched circle

Toucan

1 BELLY

Layer the three scallops to create a feathered belly.

2 BEAK

Glue the toucan beak accent as shown. Fold the beak lengthwise, then lay it flat and fold the bottom edge. Snip it in the middle to make two tabs. Then, fold the beak again so the tabs stick out.

3 EYES

Create eyes by gluing pieces in this order, from bottom to top: large circle, medium circle, iris, and pupil.

4 WINGS

Fold the leaves as shown and glue one to each side for wings.

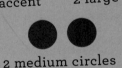

5 ALL TOGETHER

Finally, glue on the belly, beak, and eyes!

27

FROZEN FRIENDS

Penguin

1 FACE

Turn one muzzle upside-down, and glue it to another muzzle that's right side up so they overlap. Glue a diamond to the dip where they meet, and then glue a pupil on each side.

2 BODY

Add the two teardrops to each side of the lantern to create wings.

YOU WILL NEED

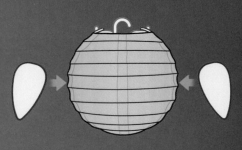

x2
2 muzzles

1 diamond

2 pupils

x2
2 teardrops

3 ALL TOGETHER

Glue the face between the wings. Your penguin is ready for a snowball fight!

Whale

1 TAIL

Fold the fin along the lines as shown, and glue it to the back of the lantern to make the whale's tale.

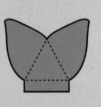

2 BALEEN

Glue whiskers that go from the mouth to the bottom of the lantern to create baleen (the stuff your whale has instead of teeth). Tuck the loose ends inside the lantern. Glue the wave to the middle of the front of the lantern for a great, big smile.

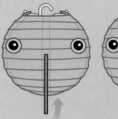
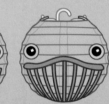

3 FLIPPERS

Fold the flippers as shown and glue the tabs to each side of the lantern.

4 SPOUT

Add bits of tissue paper to the top of the frame thingy to create a spout.

YOU WILL NEED

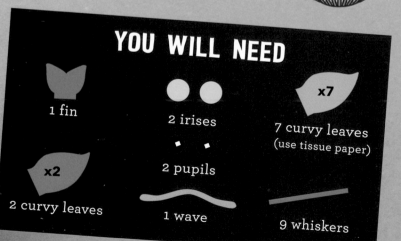

1 fin

2 irises

x7
7 curvy leaves
(use tissue paper)

x2
2 curvy leaves

2 pupils

1 wave

9 whiskers

Walrus

Change the shapes a little bit to turn your walrus into a slap-happy seal.

1 EYES

Glue a pupil onto each iris.

2 MUZZLE

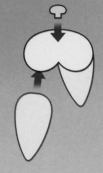

Glue the mushroom nose on the muzzle. Add the teardrops underneath to create tusks.

3 ALL TOGETHER

Glue the muzzle to the lantern first, then add the eyes and eyebrows.

Unicorn

This one takes a little time, but what do you expect? Unicorns don't come easily.

1 EARS

Fold along the curvy leaves as shown.

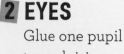

2 EYES

Glue one pupil to each iris.

3 SNOUT

Assemble the snout by bringing the two sides together and gluing the middle flap down on top.

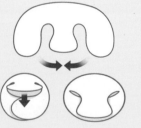

4 FACE

Run a line of glue around the inside of the snout, and then hold it onto the lantern until it dries. Then glue on the eyes and ears.

YOU WILL NEED

x2
2 curvy leaves

2 irises

2 pupils

1 teardrop

x13
13 curvy leaves
(use tissue paper)

1 snout

5 MANE

Add curvy leaves of tissue paper to the front to create a forelock. Keep adding tissue paper down the side, behind the ear. Fold the teardrop back to make the horn, and glue it between the ears.